KEITH BRUMPTON

*A special thank you to Holly McEwan
for her help in thinking up bad jokes*

Text and Illustrations copyright © Keith Brumpton 1998

First Published in Great Britain in 1998
by Macdonald Young Books
an imprint of Wayland Publishers Ltd
61 Western Road
Hove
East Sussex
BN3 1JD

Find Macdonald Young Books on the internet at
http://www.myb.co.uk

The right of Keith Brumpton to be identified
as the author and the illustrator of this Work
has been asserted by him in accordance with the
Copyright, Designs and Patents Act 1988.

Designed and Typeset by Backup Creative Services, Dorset DT10 1DB.
Printed and bound in Belgium by Proost International Book Production.

British Library Cataloguing in Publication Data available.

ISBN: 0 7500 2566 2

Chapter One – Up, Up and Away

Even superheroes need holidays. Tanya, Hoofed Crusader, had been on duty at her farm in Uddersfield for almost two years, so it was no surprise she felt the need to put away her cape and take a break.

To make it a real holiday she wasn't even going to do the flying herself. She'd decided to let the plane take the strain.

Tanya arrived at Hornsea Airport dressed in a long summer dress, a pair of trendy platform hooves, and wearing her favourite perfume, Cow-lvin Klein 'Vache' ™.

She also wore some sunglasses so that she wouldn't be recognized. (The services of superheroes are very much in demand, so it is always a good idea to remain in disguise).

Even so, being a very caring cow, Tanya had left a telephone number with her best friend Dr Rook. This was to be used only in case of emergencies, but fortunately she'd heard nothing so far. It looked like the holiday could begin in earnest!

bit of a crush

MOO YORK was fun. Tanya liked big cities. There were so few cows around it felt very peaceful.

The highlight was rollerblading in Central Park.

In MEXICOW, Tanya saw the famous Aztec temples. They were beautiful to look at, but difficult to climb wearing platform hooves.

MOSCOW was very cold. Tanya bought a fake fur hat, but her horns and ears still felt the chill.

no, not earings, they're icicles!

It was late one afternoon on Moscow's main street when Tanya's mobile phone began to ring. She reached into her bag and pulled up the phone's receiver.

"Croak. It's me"

"Dr Rook?"

"Croak. How did you guess? No, never mind that... No time... It's expensive calling Moscow and I can only carry so many pound coins in my beak... This is an emergency."

"Are you sure? You don't just mean that Uddersfield Town are losing 2-0 at half-time?"

"Croak. Don't be silly. I wouldn't spoil your holiday for a little thing like that. No... we've got real trouble down on the farm... We're talking Unidentified Furry Objects... Strange lights in the night sky!!! Tanya, the rest of the herd is terrified, you've got to come home at once...

* The biggest sort a Superhero can face.

BEEP-BEEP-BEEP…

Dr Rook's coins had run out. Tanya put away her mobile and thought for a moment.

"Unidentified Furry Objects? Sounds interesting. But it'll mean the end of my holidays… and it was Moo Zealand next. Oh well, if there are animals in trouble then it's my job to help. Time to find a telephone booth!"

man looking like a poodle

Chapter Two –
Mooing, Mooing, Gone!

Tanya wasn't quite sure the usual magic
would work inside a Russian telephone
booth. She opened the door, squeezed
inside and dialled 2-2-2. Then she waited...

There was a long delay. Then, in the
distance, there was a low rumble – the
sound of an approaching storm. That was
a good sign. There were flashes of
lightning overhead and Tanya felt a
familiar warm glow over her body.
The bell around her neck rang out,
tolling gently, Ting… Ting… Ting.

Tanya was transformed! She flew out from the telephone booth, the cold air sweeping past her outstretched hooves, up into the icy grey sky. Tanya, Hoofed Crusader, was on her way home.

Airline pilots got a terrible shock as the Caped Cow flew past...

Birds in flight had never seen anything so big move so fast.

She flew high over mountains...

And low over beaches...

Finally the landscape grew more familiar. She could see the glue factory at Hornsea, the floodlights at Uddersfield Town's ground (they were losing 4-0), the dairy at Goldtop-by-the-Wibble.

And for the first time Tanya began to wonder about the mystery which had ended her holidays and brought her speeding back home. Dr. Rook was not a crow to panic. If he thought this was an emergency then it must be serious indeed.

Unidentified Furry Objects? Strange lights in the skies? It all sounded too spooky for words and Tanya guessed that this might be the greatest challenge she'd ever faced...

Chapter Three – Something afoot at Owlhoot Farm

Much as she wanted to put her hooves up for a while, and eat some clover, there wasn't time. Tanya was met at the landing strip by Dr Rook who recounted recent events while she got changed. (As far as the other cows on the farm were concerned, Tanya was just another member of the dairy herd).

Croak. Yes. All the trouble is up in the hills. The starlings there have been complaining about UFOs moving about in the trees.

Tanya knew the starlings. They were reliable witnesses, not easily startled.

"And even worse, trees have been falling during the night… Crashing to the ground… The forest is gradually disappearing, being torn down, and yet we never see anyone there… "

Tanya swished her tail uneasily.

UFOs

I wish she'd stop doing that!

Cows don't really like forest, they prefer the open fields. But Tanya knew how important the trees were to other animals, and how they provided shade and shelter.

"OK, Doctor," she began, quietly. "Leave it with me for the moment. I think I have a plan, but first I want to see what everyone at Owlhoot Farm is saying about this business. I'll call you in the morning."

Now as it happened the rest of the cows were in a bit of a state over events. Mavis and Beryl wanted Ron the Bull to do something.

"Ladies, ladies," yawned Ron, who'd just got up from his sun-bed, "there's nothing to be afraid of. I'm here to protect you aren't I?"

(He flexed his neck muscles and Mavis and Beryl were thrilled.)

"I'm too busy to be bothered with all this nonsense while I'm trying to organize next Saturday's line dancing contest. Which of you lovely ladies will partner me, I wonder?"

Mavis and Beryl and the rest of the herd were so excited to hear about the dance contest they soon forgot all about the UFOs and the falling trees.

But that same night, as Tanya lay in her hay trying to think of a plan, ten more trees were felled, and in the forest all was not well...

Chapter Four – Bale-watch

Imagine a dark, misty evening, with
the moon half-hidden by clouds.
Good, that's saved me
from having
to describe
it to you…

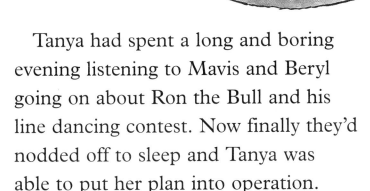

Tanya had spent a long and boring
evening listening to Mavis and Beryl
going on about Ron the Bull and his
line dancing contest. Now finally they'd
nodded off to sleep and Tanya was
able to put her plan into operation.

Sneaking out of the barn, she crossed the muddy tracks, vaulted the stone wall, and made her way towards the lonely public call box where she was quickly transformed into... the Caped Cow!

Tanya used her magical powers to swiftly fly herself in the direction of Wetpeak Woods, where the forest stood dim and still, like Uddersfield Town's centre-half.

Tanya plucked off a couple of branches and disguised herself as a tree.

Hope my horns don't give the game away!

It wasn't one of her better disguises. She waited. The forest was as silent as two goldfish singing 'Silent Night'. At first Tanya saw nothing especially mysterious: two badgers travelling home from a late night disco.

Hi, Tanya! Like the disguise...

Two fireflies danced overhead, and then an elderly frog with a limp.

Evening, Tanya. Nice branch.

The mist grew denser, Tanya's tail began to get cold. What if Dr Rook had been wrong and there were no UFOs, no falling trees? It may all have been a wild rook chase.

came a sound from the distance. It was a mechanical, grinding sound, and Tanya moved quickly into action.

Bzzz...

The noise grew closer as the Hoofed Crusader made her way through the trees, stopping every now and then to look for clues, or to check her location.

For the first time she heard the sound of falling timber. The whole forest seemed to be groaning and crying out. Something terrible was happening, and now was the time for Tanya to make herself known. She swallowed hard and suddenly, there before her, stood the enemy…

Chapter Five – Horse Code

It was a large, masked stallion, and he was clutching a chain-saw in his hooves. All around lay a pile of felled trees, dead foliage, homeless ants. The horse gave a manic laugh and introduced himself.

Tanya thought she recognized him from a neighbour's field. He was always talking nonsense to a crowd of horseflies that followed him around, but now it looked like he'd completely flipped.

"I don't know your game," began Tanya, bravely edging forward, "but this has to stop. These trees can't be replaced, you know… You're making a lot of creatures homeless."

Equus let out another crazed whinny.

"Nay, lass, you're wrong. I've no intention of stopping until I've got rid of every tree in Porkshire. Then we horses can gallop free once again, like in the good old days."

"He's mad," thought Tanya, "mad and dangerous."

Equus trotted confidently forward and challenged Tanya to combat.

Tanya had only just come back from holiday and her powers seemed a little rusty.

Before she could really get going, Equus had seized her by the hooves and left her trussed up between two tightly sprung trees. The Hoofed Crusader watched helplessly as her adversary galloped off into the woods, his chain-saw poised to do yet more damage.

"Sorry you're too tied up to join me,"
he neighed, "I'm off to Owlhoot Farm to
chop down their trees. He he hee!"

The barn! And everyone'll be asleep... they'll be flattened!

Tanya struggled, but for a horse
Equus had been very good with his knots.
In the branches above, Tanya saw a
strange dim glow. Then another. Were
these the famous UFOs of which Dr Rook
had spoken?

34

Was there no end to a cow's troubles?
And then, as she looked more closely,
Tanya could see something red and furry…
Unidentified Furry Objects. The lights drew
closer until finally she could see everything…
A group of squirrels carrying torches.

Their leader sprang forward and
introduced himself.

You're the Unidentified Furry Objects?

"Yes. Of course. We've had this Equus chap under observation for some time. Seems totally out of control. Been hoping to get a chance to help take him on. Of course he's a bit big for us."

"Then let's team up," cried Tanya. "Help me get loose and we'll get after him. I know exactly where he's headed."

In no time at all, the "Nutbusters" had nibbled through Tanya's ropes and she issued her orders to the Major and his squadron.

Chapter Six – Keep going, only a few pages left

Tanya was now in hot pursuit of Equus. She feared he might try to fell the old elm tree which stood right next to the barn. It was a huge and beautiful old tree, and if it fell… well, there'd be a lot of squashed cows.

It was too foggy to fly, so the Hoofed
Crusader donned her rollerblades and
sped along the forest track. The minutes
were ticking away but still there was no
sign of Equus up ahead. Horses could
move pretty fast when they wanted to.

It was a familiar sound. Tanya zoomed
into view in time to see Equus poised to saw
through the last section of the old elm tree.

Hoping that her powers would be back to full strength, the Hoofed Crusader swished her tail angrily and pointed it in the direction of Equus.

Out shot a powerful ray of white light stopping Equus in his tracks.

The deadly ice ray had done its trick, but the tree was just about to fall... In fact, with an awful, terrifying croak, over it went, crashing into the cattle barn with a sickening thud!

Corned beef pie!

"Take your partner by the hoof,
And wheel her round and round."

Tanya could hear music. Not from the cattle barn but from the field beyond... She rollerbladed closer, past the wreckage of her beloved barn and the beautiful old elm.

There, in the field, to her joy, stood
Ron the Bull and the rest of the herd.
They were practising their line dancing.

Tanya felt overjoyed… And puzzled.
It was left to Ron the bull to explain.
"Tanya, baby, you've missed all the
action as usual. We've been getting free
line dancing lessons from this Major
Nutbush character. He's only a squirrel,
but he knows all the steps."

"And then," interrupted Mavis excitedly, "a tree fell on our barn and we'd all have been killed if it hadn't been for Ron. Isn't he wonderful?"

All the other cows laughed. They laughed even more when they saw Tanya's rollerblades and said that the dance judges would disqualify her.

But that night as she lay in the old shed

which Terry the farmhand had prepared
for them, Tanya knew she wasn't really
alone in the world.

Dr Rook had dropped in to congratulate
her and to tell her that Equus had been
defrosted and taken away to a Welsh Pony
Trekking Centre. Squirrel Squadron 633
called by with a bouquet of flowers and
some hay, and she'd also received an
invitation to a disco next Saturday from
the badgers. Which was more like it as far
as Tanya was concerned – she'd always
preferred techno to line dancing...

Epilogue – Tanya, the Moo-vie?

Tanya took a deep breath and sat back down in her chair.

"And that's it… that's the idea for my moo-vie."

The head of the film company swivelled round in his big leather chair and puffed out his cheeks.

"Nice story, cow," he smiled. "It's a nice story. But who'd believe it? I mean… How could a cow ever be a superhero? I'm sorry."

Tanya smiled quietly to herself, shrugged her hooves and flew out through the open window.

I don't believe it! It must be done with special effects!!!

Sometimes fact is stranger than fiction. At least, that's what we cows say...

The End

Message from the Safe Book Society

Congratulations!
You have managed to finish this book
without injuring yourself. But please be
careful when closing it. Many injuries
happen to readers who get their fingers
caught between the closing pages. If in
doubt, consult an adult or librarian.

Your pet hamster is bored and asks you to read it a story. What do you choose? Why not try a Keith Brumpton book? They're the ones hamsters prefer and vets recommend.*

Tanya, Hoofed Crusader

Tanya was just an ordinary clover-loving cow, until that fateful stormy night. A flash of lightning, a clap of thunder... and Tanya the cow became TANYA, HOOFED CRUSADER!

Superheroes Gone Bust

The superheroes in Fowlmouth-under-Lime have a few problems. Elasticman loses his elasticity and goes slack under pressure. Mothgirl can't avoid bright lights, hence the plasters. And Skeletonman is very overweight for a skeleton. However, Laura is convinced that all they need is a crime to solve. Enter the Skunk...

The Four-Legged Sheriff

At high noon the Dirty Rotten Lowdown Gang is riding into town. It's up to Trigger, the four-legged sheriff, to fight the meanest baddies in the West...

Look Out, Loch Ness Monster!

For as long as he could remember, Kevin McAllister has had one ambition – to be the first person to see the Loch Ness Monster. Then one moonlit night, Kevin sees a huge shadow moving across the water. Could this really be the Loch Ness Monster at last?

You can buy all these books from your local bookseller, or they can be ordered direct from the publisher. For more information about Storybooks, write to: *The Sales Department, Macdonald Young Books, 61 Western Road, Hove, East Sussex BN3 1JD*

* Also suitable for humans, tired huskies and certain types of chipmunk.